GAM/CH

BOYS ONLY

HOW TO SURVIVE (ALMOST) ANYTHING!

BUSTER BOOKS

D0227738

ILLUSTRATED BY
SIMON ECOB

WRITTEN BY
MARTIN OLIVER

EDITED BY HANNAH COHEN
DESIGNED BY ZOE QUAYLE

DISCLAIMER
The publisher and author disclaim, as far as is legally permissible,
all liability for accidents, or injuries or loss that may occur as a result
of information or instructions given in this book.

The hints and tips in this book are intended for practice purposes only.
Under no circumstances should you ever attempt any exercise that
would put yourself or others in any danger in real life. Use your best
common sense at all times – particularly when using heat or sharp
objects – always wear appropriate safety gear, stay within the law and
local rules, and be considerate of other people. Always remember
to ask a responsible adult for assistance and take their advice
whenever necessary.

First published in Great Britain in 2012 by Buster Books,
an imprint of Michael O'Mara Books Limited,
9 Lion Yard, Tremadoc Road, London SW4 7NQ

www.busterbooks.co.uk

Copyright © Buster Books 2012

All rights reserved. No part of this publication may be reproduced, stored in a retrieval system,
or transmitted by any means, without the prior permission in writing of the publisher, nor be
otherwise circulated in any form of binding or cover other than that in which it is published and without
a similar condition including this condition being imposed on the subsequent purchaser.

A CIP catalogue record for this book is available from the British Library.

ISBN: 978-1-907151-98-9

1 3 5 7 9 10 8 6 4 2

Papers used by Michael O'Mara Books are natural, recyclable products
made from wood grown in sustainable forests. The manufacturing processes
conform to the environmental regulations of the country of origin.

This book was printed in April 2012 by Shenzhen Wing King Tong Paper Products Co. Ltd.,
Shenzhen, Guangdong, China.

CONTENTS

WARNING!

NOT READING THIS BOOK COULD BE SERIOUSLY BAD FOR YOUR HEALTH.

HOW WOULD YOU COPE IF THE BOAT YOU WERE ON SUDDENLY STARTED SINKING? OR IF YOU CAME FACE-TO-FACE WITH AN ANGRY CROCODILE?

WHEN ONE FALSE MOVE COULD PROVE DISASTROUS, THERE'S ONE PIECE OF KIT THAT COULD TURN OUT TO BE A LIFESAVER ... THIS BOOK! READING IT MIGHT JUST BE THE SMARTEST THING YOU'VE EVER DONE.

SIMPLY FOLLOW THE ADVICE OF THESE BOYS, AND BE PROPERLY PREPARED TO FACE WHATEVER UNEXPECTED ADVENTURES LIFE MAY THROW AT YOU ...

ARE YOU READY?

HAVING THE RIGHT KIT WILL GIVE YOU A HEAD START IN YOUR BID TO STAY ALIVE.

POCKET PACK

SWING THE SURVIVAL BALANCE IN YOUR FAVOUR BY ALWAYS CARRYING A FEW ABSOLUTE ESSENTIALS IN A SMALL TIN:

- A MIRROR (FOR SIGNALLING)
- A NEEDLE AND THREAD
- A FISH-HOOK AND LINE
- A COMPASS
- A SMALL FIRST-AID KIT, INCLUDING PLASTERS AND INSECT REPELLANT.

THE BEST POCKET PACKS ARE SMALL, LIGHTWEIGHT AND WATERPROOF.

SURVIVAL BACKPACK

IF YOU'RE ABLE TO PREPARE FOR AN EXPEDITION IN ADVANCE, CHOOSE A STURDY, WATERPROOF BACKPACK AND PACK THESE EXTRA ITEMS:

- FUEL • A TORCH
- FOOD AND WATER SUPPLIES • A KNIFE
- ROPE OR STRING • SUN CREAM
- A COMPLETE FIRST-AID KIT
- WATER PURIFYING TABLETS
- A SLEEPING BAG/SURVIVAL BLANKET
- WATERPROOFS • A RADIO
- SIGNALLING EQUIPMENT, SUCH AS FLARES
- A CHANGE OF CLOTHING
- A PLASTIC BAG.

NOW TURN THE PAGE AND DISCOVER HOW TO SURVIVE ALMOST ANYTHING!

HOW TO SURVIVE A SHARK ATTACK

SHARK ATTACKS ARE RARE, BUT IF YOU DO HAPPEN TO FIND YOURSELF
IN SHARK-INFESTED WATERS, STICK TO THIS ADVICE.

KEEP CLOSE TO OTHER SWIMMERS – SHARKS ARE LESS
LIKELY TO ATTACK MORE THAN ONE PERSON.

SHARK!

STOP SPLASHING
AROUND – IT WILL
THINK YOU'RE
A FISH!

IF YOU DO SPOT
A SHARK FIN ABOVE
THE WATER, SWIM
BACK TO THE BEACH
AS CALMLY AS
POSSIBLE.

DITCH SHINY ITEMS – THESE
LOOK LIKE TASTY FISH SCALES
TO A SHARK.

THAT RING
HAS TO GO.

BLOOD ATTRACTS SHARKS, SO DON'T
SWIM WITH GRAZES OR OPEN WOUNDS
AND TAKE CARE NOT TO CUT YOURSELF
IN OPEN WATER.

UH, OH ...

AS YOU HEAD TO SAFETY, USE ANIMAL TRACKS TO GUIDE YOU TO WATERING HOLES AND FEEDING PLACES. BUT WATCH OUT FOR THE ANIMALS THEMSELVES!

FOR THE FIRST FEW DAYS, IT'S MORE IMPORTANT TO FIND WATER THAN FOOD.

LEAVE A T-SHIRT OUT OVERNIGHT OR OUT IN THE RAIN TO SOAK UP DEW OR RAINWATER, THEN WRING IT INTO A CUP FOR A REFRESHING DRINK.

ALWAYS BOIL WATER FROM PONDS OR PUDDLES BEFORE DRINKING IT TO KILL ANY BUGS.

BEING HUNGRY BUT HEALTHY IS BETTER THAN BEING ILL, SO ONLY EAT FOOD THAT YOU KNOW IS SAFE.

BETTER NOT RISK EATING THESE BERRIES.

HOW TO SURVIVE FROSTBITE

WHEN YOU'RE OUT IN THE COLD, FROSTBITE IS ENEMY NUMBER ONE.
HERE'S HOW TO SPOT IT AND DEAL WITH IT.

WHAT IS FROSTBITE?

FROSTBITE IS WHEN YOUR SKIN AND FLESH LITERALLY FREEZE.

IT ATTACKS AREAS WITH THE LEAST BLOOD CIRCULATION - YOUR HANDS, FACE AND TOES.

ER, WHAT DO YOU LOOK LIKE?!?

I'M MOVING MY FACE TO KEEP THE CIRCULATION GOING.

SKIN FIRST GOES RED AND PRICKLY, THEN WAXY-LOOKING PATCHES OF GREY FORM.

THAT DOESN'T LOOK GOOD ...

IF FROSTBITE STRIKES IN YOUR HANDS, REMOVE WET GLOVES, THEN WARM YOUR HANDS UNDER YOUR ARMPITS.

BE WARNED - THAWING FROSTBITE IS PAINFUL!

HOW TO SURVIVE A PLANE CRASH

FOLLOWING THE ADVICE ON THESE PAGES WILL INCREASE YOUR CHANCES OF SURVIVAL IF YOU DO FIND YOURSELF IN A FALLING AIRCRAFT.

BEFORE TAKE OFF, LISTEN CAREFULLY TO THE SAFETY ANNOUNCEMENTS.

FASTEN YOUR SEAT BELT.

PRACTISE THE 'BRACE POSITION' - IT'S THE SAFEST POSITION TO BE IN ON IMPACT. CUSHION YOUR HEAD ON THE SEAT IN FRONT OR REST YOUR HEAD ON YOUR KNEES AND HOLD YOUR LEGS IF THERE ISN'T A SEAT IN FRONT OF YOU.

REMOVE ANY SHARP ITEMS FROM YOUR POCKETS.

RELAX AND ENJOY THE FLIGHT, EVERYONE!

ONCE OUTSIDE, MOVE AWAY FROM THE PLANE - THERE MAY STILL BE DANGER FROM FIRE.

HELP ANY INJURED PEOPLE.

ARE YOU OKAY?

WHEN YOU'RE SURE THERE'S NO CHANCE OF A FIRE OR EXPLOSION, SEARCH THE WRECKAGE FOR SURVIVAL ITEMS, SUCH AS FOOD AND SHELTER EQUIPMENT.

HELP RESCUERS TO FIND YOU BY REMAINING NEAR THE CRASH SITE - IT SHOULD BE EASILY VISIBLE FROM THE AIR - AND SET UP DISTRESS SIGNALS, TOO.

WE NEED THREE FIRES IN A TRIANGLE - THAT'S THE INTERNATIONAL SIGN FOR BEING IN TROUBLE.

USE WRECKAGE OR CLOTHING TO MAKE AN 'X' AND A TRIANGLE ON THE GROUND. RESCUERS KNOW THAT 'X' MEANS MEDICAL ASSISTANCE IS NEEDED. A TRIANGLE TELLS THEM IT SHOULD BE SAFE TO LAND.

GREAT WORK, GUYS!

I'VE SPOTTED THEM. LOOKS LIKE THERE ARE CASUALTIES.

HOW TO SURVIVE IN THE DESERT

IF YOU'RE LOST IN THE DESERT, THE FIRST THING TO DO IS FIND SHELTER FROM THE SUN.

LOOK FOR SHADOWS CAST BY TREES, BUSHES OR ROCKS AND STAY THERE DURING THE HEAT OF THE DAY.

WHEN NIGHT FALLS, MAKE A SHELTER BY DRAPING MATERIAL OVER A LARGE ROCK OR TREE BRANCH. PILE SMALLER ROCKS AROUND THE EDGES TO KEEP THE WIND OUT.

YOUR BIGGEST DANGER IS LACK OF WATER - WITHOUT IT YOU WILL LAST ONLY TWO AND A HALF DAYS!

CREATE YOUR OWN SOURCE OF WATER BY MAKING AN EMERGENCY SOLAR STILL. HERE'S HOW:

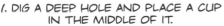

1. DIG A DEEP HOLE AND PLACE A CUP IN THE MIDDLE OF IT.

2. SURROUND THE OUTSIDE OF THE CUP WITH SPONGY BITS OF PLANT.

3. CUT A PLASTIC BAG ALONG ONE SEAM AND ALONG THE BOTTOM EDGE TO MAKE A PLASTIC SHEET.

4. COVER THE HOLE WITH THE PLASTIC SHEET. SECURE IT USING ROCKS. PLACE A STONE IN THE MIDDLE, DIRECTLY ABOVE THE CUP.

5. THROUGHOUT THE DAY, WATER VAPOUR WILL DRIP INTO THE CUP - ENOUGH FOR A SMALL DRINK, BUT NOT ENOUGH WATER TO KEEP YOU ALIVE FOR LONG.

CONSERVE BODY FLUIDS BY KEEPING YOUR MOVEMENTS SLOW AND SMALL TO PREVENT SWEATING.

TRAVEL DURING THE NIGHT WHEN IT IS MUCH COOLER TO FIND OTHER SOURCES OF WATER.

17

HOW TO AVOID A POLAR BEAR ATTACK

IF YOU'RE TREKKING IN BEAR COUNTRY, YOU'LL NEED TO STICK TO THESE RULES TO AVOID BECOMING BEAR BRUNCH!

AVOID ATTRACTING THE ATTENTION OF A POLAR BEAR BY KEEPING A CLEAN CAMP - BEARS CAN SNIFF FOOD SMELLS FROM A LONG WAY AWAY.

STAY AWAY FROM MAMMAL CARCASSES. POLAR BEARS ARE SCAVENGERS AND WILL BE ATTRACTED TO THE PROSPECT OF A FREE MEAL.

NEVER PET A POLAR BEAR CUB - ITS MOTHER WON'T LIKE IT AND MAY BE HIDING JUST AROUND THE CORNER!

IF YOU'RE UNLUCKY ENOUGH TO BE APPROACHED BY A POLAR BEAR, STAND YOUR GROUND. IT MAY THINK YOU LOOK LIKE TOO MUCH BOTHER TO ATTACK COMPARED TO A TEENY, TINY SEAL PUP.

MAKE YOURSELF LOOK AS BIG AND SCARY AS POSSIBLE BY STANDING TALL AND HOLDING A JACKET OVER YOUR HEAD.

IF THIS DOESN'T WORK, SHOUT LOUDLY AT THE BEAR TO SCARE IT OFF.

YAH!

WHATEVER YOU DO, DON'T RUN AWAY - A BEAR WILL ALWAYS OUTRUN YOU!

HOW TO SURVIVE A FLASH FLOOD

HOW TO TREAT A BROKEN LEG

IF ONE OF YOUR TEAM WAS FACED WITH AN INJURY SUCH AS A BROKEN LEG, HOW WOULD YOU TREAT IT? READ ON TO FIND OUT.

PAIN, TENDERNESS AND SWELLING ARE SIGNS OF A BROKEN BONE. DON'T MOVE IT AND SEEK MEDICAL ATTENTION AT ONCE.

IF YOU ARE STUCK OUT IN THE WILD, FOLLOW THESE STEPS:

DON'T PUT ANYTHING ON THE WOUND, HOWEVER, IF IT'S BLEEDING HEAVILY APPLY STEADY PRESSURE USING A STERILE BANDAGE TO STOP THE FLOW.

IT'S OKAY, YOU'RE NOT BLEEDING.

FIND TWO SIMILAR-SIZED LENGTHS OF WOOD TO MAKE A SPLINT - THIS HELPS THE BROKEN BONES STAY IN PLACE.

HOW TO SURVIVE AN EARTHQUAKE

EARTHQUAKES OCCUR WHEN ROCKS IN THE EARTH'S CRUST MOVE, CAUSING THE GROUND ABOVE TO SHAKE. FOLLOW THIS ADVICE TO INCREASE YOUR CHANCES OF SURVIVAL IF ONE HITS.

IF YOU'RE IN AN EARTHQUAKE ZONE, LISTEN OUT FOR WARNING REPORTS.

IF YOU HAVE ADVANCE WARNING OF A STRIKE, TURN OFF GAS AND ELECTRICITY SUPPLIES – DURING AN EARTHQUAKE THEY COULD CAUSE A FIRE.

IF A QUAKE STRIKES ...

... STAY INDOORS! AVOID OBJECTS THAT COULD FALL ON YOU AND FIND A STURDY PIECE OF FURNITURE TO SHELTER BENEATH.

STAY AWAY FROM WINDOWS THAT MIGHT SHATTER.

HOW TO SURVIVE A FOREST FIRE

FOREST FIRES ARE UNPREDICTABLE AND CAN IGNITE WITH ALMOST NO WARNING. FOLLOW THESE RULES AND BE READY IF ONE STRIKES.

IF YOU'RE STAYING IN AN AREA AT RISK, KEEP AN EYE ON LOCAL NEWS FOR FIRE WARNINGS.

IF A FIRE IS REPORTED, CLEAR VEGETATION AND FLAMMABLE MATERIALS WITHIN 11 METRES OF YOUR HOUSE. SOAK THE GROUND WITH WATER, TOO.

TURN OFF ALL GAS SUPPLIES. THEN PLAN AN EXIT ROUTE. TRAVEL LIGHT AND FAST.

IF YOU NEED TO EVACUATE, PUT ON LONG SLEEVES AND TROUSERS. PLACE A WET HANDKERCHIEF OVER YOUR MOUTH AND SOAK A BLANKET IN WATER TO TAKE WITH YOU.

HOW TO SURVIVE IN A WHITEOUT

DURING A BLIZZARD, VISIBILITY CAN BECOME SO BAD THAT WHITE CLOUD AND SNOWY GROUND REFLECT MOST OF THE AVAILABLE LIGHT. THIS IS CALLED A WHITEOUT. IT'S EASY TO BECOME DISORIENTATED, SO FOLLOW THIS ADVICE.

WATCH OUT FOR LOOMING, LOW, DARK CLOUDS AND AN INCREASE IN THE WIND – A BLIZZARD MAY BE APPROACHING.

IF A BLIZZARD BEGINS, HEAD FOR THE SHELTER OF BOULDERS, CAVES OR TREES.

IF A WHITEOUT OCCURS, REMAIN WHERE YOU ARE – IF YOU MOVE AROUND YOU COULD GET LOST OR FALL INTO RAVINES HIDDEN BY THE SNOW.

TURN YOUR BACK TO THE WIND AND COVER YOUR MOUTH, NOSE AND EYES TO KEEP FREEZING AIR OUT.

HOW TO SURVIVE A ZOMBIE INVASION

IF YOUR TOWN IS INVADED BY ZOMBIES – OR THE 'UNDEAD' AS THEY PREFER TO BE KNOWN – YOU WILL NEED A PLAN ... FAST!

SPOTTING A ZOMBIE IS SIMPLE – THEY WALK SLOWLY AND JERKILY, DROOL SALIVA AND ARE OFTEN DIRTY AND COVERED IN WEEPING WOUNDS.

ZOMBIES FEED ON LIVING FLESH AND WILL BE LOOKING FOR YOU, SO YOU WILL NEED TO MAKE A SECURE BASE.

A BASE IS THE PERFECT PLACE TO STORE FOOD AND TEAM UP WITH OTHER SURVIVORS.

UNFORTUNATELY, IT MAY EVENTUALLY ATTRACT HORDES OF ZOMBIES WHO CAN SMELL FRESH MEAT.

KNOW YOUR EXITS. IF ZOMBIES HAVE SNIFFED YOU OUT, ABANDON YOUR BASE AND FIND ANOTHER.

ERR ... IT'S TIME TO MOVE ON, GUYS, LET'S LEAVE BY THE BACK WAY.

CHECK STRANGERS FOR CUTS OR BITES. IF A ZOMBIE BREAKS THE SKIN OF ITS VICTIM, IT'S ONLY A MATTER OF TIME UNTIL THEY TURN INTO ZOMBIES THEMSELVES.

WHEN ON THE MOVE, STAY ALERT. CARRY SAUSAGES TO USE AS A DISTRACTION IF YOU NEED TO.

IF YOU BUMP INTO A ZOMBIE, RUN! THEY ARE PRETTY SLOW.

WEAR BODY ARMOUR TO PROTECT AGAINST ZOMBIE BITES AND SCRATCHES.

IF YOU'RE AMBUSHED OR CAN'T ESCAPE ... USE A BIT OF BRAIN POWER!

ADOPT A ZOMBIE POSE AND SHUFFLE SLOWLY.

RIP YOUR CLOTHES AND SMEAR DIRT OVER YOUR SKIN.

DRIBBLE AND ROAR, THEN WANDER OFF WHEN NO ONE'S LOOKING.

ZOMBIES ARE ALREADY TECHNICALLY DEAD, SO SHOOTING THEM OR HACKING OFF A LIMB WILL ONLY SLOW THEM DOWN. INSTEAD, WHACK THEM AS HARD AS YOU CAN ON THEIR HEAD TO FINISH THEM OFF.

WASH AWAY ANY VENOM LEFT ON THE SKIN WITH WATER AND SOAP IF POSSIBLE.

WRAP A SINGLE BANDAGE ABOVE THE BITE, AND THEN OVER THE BITE ITSELF. THE BANDAGE SLOWS THE FLOW OF BLOOD THROUGH THE BODY, WHICH SLOWS THE MOVEMENT OF THE VENOM.

DON'T WRAP THE BANDAGE TOO TIGHT.

NEVER CUT THE FLESH AROUND THE BITE AND SUCK OUT THE VENOM. THIS MAY ONLY SPREAD THE VENOM AND CAUSE INFECTION.

KEEP THE VICTIM AS STILL AND CALM AS POSSIBLE UNTIL HELP ARRIVES.

GET A GOOD GRIP ON YOUR COMPANION, SO THAT WHEN HIS PARACHUTE OPENS AND HE STARTS TO FALL MORE SLOWLY, THE FORCE OF IT DOESN'T PULL YOU OFF.

BRACE YOURSELF! THE FORCE OF A PARACHUTE OPENING WITH YOUR COMBINED WEIGHTS COULD DISLOCATE YOUR SHOULDERS OR BREAK YOUR ARMS.

HOLD ON TIGHT TO MY SHOULDER STRAPS, I'M ABOUT TO OPEN MY PARACHUTE ...

ONCE THE CANOPY OF THE PARACHUTE IS OPEN, TRY TO LAND ON WATER. AFTER LANDING, QUICKLY HELP EACH OTHER TO SHORE BEFORE YOUR PARACHUTES FILL WITH WATER AND GET TOO HEAVY TO LIFT.

IF THERE IS NO WATER AROUND, LOOK FOR A PLOUGHED FIELD TO LAND ON INSTEAD.

LAND ON YOUR FEET AND ROLL TO MINIMIZE IMPACT.

I CAN SEE ONE. IT'S GOING TO BE A ROUGH LANDING!

HANG ON, BUDDY, NEARLY THERE ...

HOW TO SURVIVE A CROC ATTACK

CROCODILES ARE AWESOME PREDATORS. THEY LIVE IN SALT WATER OR FRESH WATER AND CAN GROW TO OVER SIX METRES LONG. TO SURVIVE AN ATTACK, KNOW AS MUCH AS POSSIBLE ABOUT THEM.

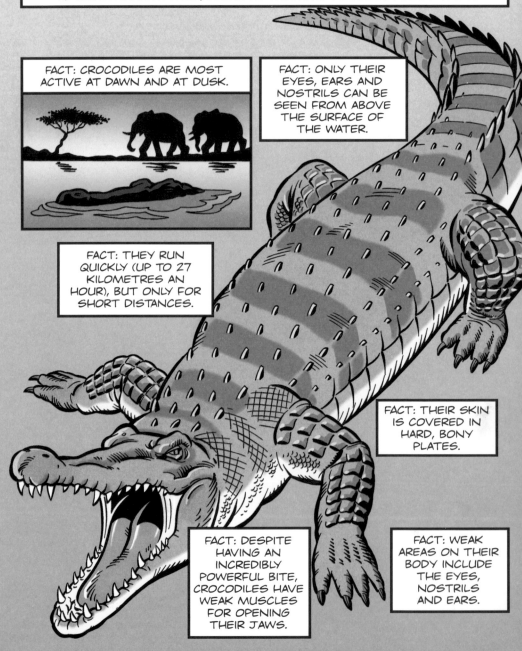

FACT: CROCODILES ARE MOST ACTIVE AT DAWN AND AT DUSK.

FACT: ONLY THEIR EYES, EARS AND NOSTRILS CAN BE SEEN FROM ABOVE THE SURFACE OF THE WATER.

FACT: THEY RUN QUICKLY (UP TO 27 KILOMETRES AN HOUR), BUT ONLY FOR SHORT DISTANCES.

FACT: THEIR SKIN IS COVERED IN HARD, BONY PLATES.

FACT: DESPITE HAVING AN INCREDIBLY POWERFUL BITE, CROCODILES HAVE WEAK MUSCLES FOR OPENING THEIR JAWS.

FACT: WEAK AREAS ON THEIR BODY INCLUDE THE EYES, NOSTRILS AND EARS.

SECRET WEAK SPOT: THE PALATAL VALVE - A FLAP JUST BEHIND THE TONGUE THAT COVERS THEIR THROATS WHEN SUBMERGED, SO THEY DON'T DROWN UNDERWATER.

HOW TO SURVIVE A LIGHTNING STRIKE

LIGHTNING STRIKES ARE UNPREDICTABLE, FAST AND POTENTIALLY FATAL. THE BEST WAY TO SURVIVE ONE IS TO AVOID IT IN THE FIRST PLACE. HERE'S HOW:

IF THUNDER FOLLOWS LIGHTNING BY LESS THAN 30 SECONDS, YOU ARE IN THE MIDDLE OF THE STORM AND IT IS TIME TO ACT.

IT'S TIME TO MOVE GUYS.

IF YOU CAN, SEEK SHELTER IN A LARGE, BRICK-BUILT BUILDING.

CAN WE REACH THAT BUILDING IN TIME?

IT'S TOO FAR AWAY – WE'LL BE TOO EXPOSED TO STRIKES IF WE MAKE A RUN FOR IT.

NO WAY, THEY COULD EASILY GET STRUCK BY LIGHTNING.

WHAT ABOUT SHELTERING BY THOSE CARS?

SO WHERE CAN WE GO?

AVOID METAL OBJECTS!

THESE ACT AS 'CONDUCTORS' THAT THE LIGHTNING'S ELECTRIC CHARGE CAN TRAVEL THROUGH. IF YOU TOUCH A CONDUCTOR THAT HAS BEEN STRUCK BY LIGHTNING, THE CURRENT WILL TRAVEL THROUGH YOU, TOO.

IF YOU'RE STUCK OUT IN THE OPEN, STAY THERE, BUT DON'T ...

... GO NEAR PYLONS ...

... OR PUT UP AN UMBRELLA ...

... OR SHELTER UNDER TALL TREES WHICH ARE MORE LIKELY TO GET STRUCK BY LIGHTNING.

INSTEAD, GET INTO THE LIGHTNING SAFETY CROUCH TO STAY ALIVE:

TAKE OFF YOUR WATCH AND ANY METAL ITEMS. THROW THEM FAR AWAY FROM YOU.

CROUCH DOWN AND COVER YOUR EARS WITH YOUR HANDS TO PROTECT THEM FROM THUNDER.

STAY IN THE CROUCH POSITION UNTIL THE STORM HAS PASSED BEFORE GETTING UP AND HEADING FOR SHELTER.

STAY DOWN!!

HOW TO SURVIVE A T-REX

IMAGINE BEING ZAPPED BACK IN TIME OVER 65 MILLION YEARS AND SPOTTING A DEADLY PREHISTORIC PREDATOR – A TYRANNOSAURUS REX! FOLLOW THESE TIPS TO STAY ALIVE.

DO STAY ALERT – AT UP TO SIX METRES TALL, T-REXES WERE EASY TO SPOT, BUT THEY MAY HAVE SURPRISED PREY BY ATTACKING THEM FROM THE BUSHES.

DON'T ASSUME THERE IS ONLY ONE, EITHER ... T-REXES MAY HAVE HUNTED LARGER PREY IN PACKS.

DON'T STAY PUT AND PLAY DEAD – T-REXES HAD AN EXCELLENT SENSE OF SMELL TO SNIFF OUT THEIR NEXT MEAL.

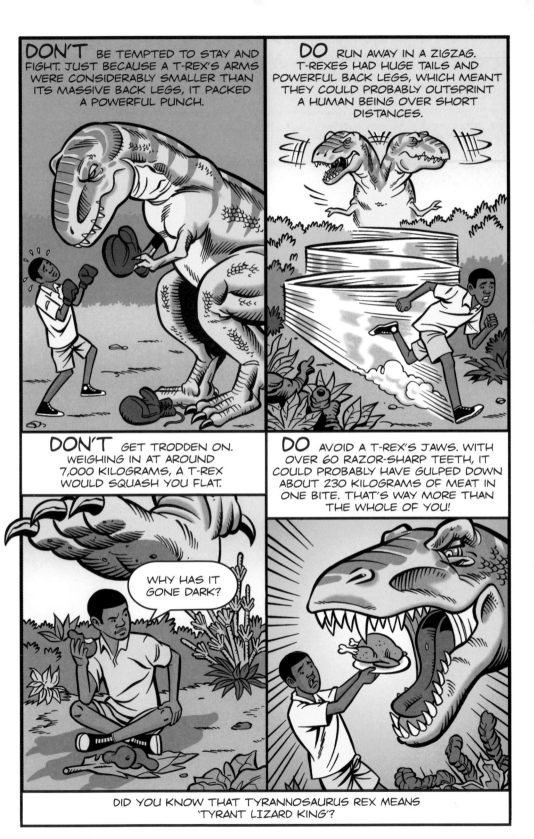

DON'T BE TEMPTED TO STAY AND FIGHT. JUST BECAUSE A T-REX'S ARMS WERE CONSIDERABLY SMALLER THAN ITS MASSIVE BACK LEGS, IT PACKED A POWERFUL PUNCH.

DO RUN AWAY IN A ZIGZAG. T-REXES HAD HUGE TAILS AND POWERFUL BACK LEGS, WHICH MEANT THEY COULD PROBABLY OUTSPRINT A HUMAN BEING OVER SHORT DISTANCES.

DON'T GET TRODDEN ON. WEIGHING IN AT AROUND 7,000 KILOGRAMS, A T-REX WOULD SQUASH YOU FLAT.

DO AVOID A T-REX'S JAWS. WITH OVER 60 RAZOR-SHARP TEETH, IT COULD PROBABLY HAVE GULPED DOWN ABOUT 230 KILOGRAMS OF MEAT IN ONE BITE. THAT'S WAY MORE THAN THE WHOLE OF YOU!

WHY HAS IT GONE DARK?

DID YOU KNOW THAT TYRANNOSAURUS REX MEANS 'TYRANT LIZARD KING'?

41

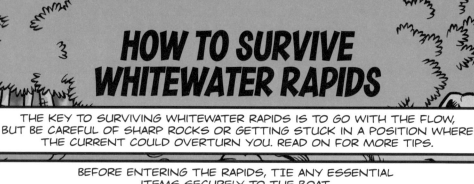

HOW TO SURVIVE WHITEWATER RAPIDS

THE KEY TO SURVIVING WHITEWATER RAPIDS IS TO GO WITH THE FLOW, BUT BE CAREFUL OF SHARP ROCKS OR GETTING STUCK IN A POSITION WHERE THE CURRENT COULD OVERTURN YOU. READ ON FOR MORE TIPS.

BEFORE ENTERING THE RAPIDS, TIE ANY ESSENTIAL ITEMS SECURELY TO THE BOAT.

HOLD ON TO YOUR HELMETS, GUYS, IT'S ABOUT TO GET BUMPY!

GRIP YOUR PADDLE WITH ONE HAND OVER THE TOP AND THE OTHER DOWN NEAR THE BLADE.

GRIP THE BOAT WITH YOUR FEET, TOO!

YOU NEED TO WORK TOGETHER AS A TEAM TO KEEP THE BOAT AS EVENLY BALANCED AS POSSIBLE AT ALL TIMES.

NOW ALL TOGETHER, TEAM, PADDLE!

THE RIDER AT THE BACK OF THE BOAT NEEDS TO USE HIS PADDLE TO STEER THE BOAT AND SHOUT INSTRUCTIONS TO THE TEAM.

IF YOU END UP OVERBOARD ...

... FLOAT DOWN RIVER FEET FIRST, AS NEAR TO THE SURFACE AS POSSIBLE TO AVOID ROCKS UNDERNEATH.

USE YOUR PADDLE TO HELP YOU FLOAT AND TO HELP OTHERS HAUL YOU BACK IN.

THANKS!

HOW TO SURVIVE A SINKING SHIP

HOW TO SURVIVE A VAMPIRE ATTACK

STRONG, SUPER-FAST AND BLOODTHIRSTY - YOU DON'T WANT TO TANGLE WITH A VAMPIRE UNLESS YOU'RE PROPERLY PREPARED ...

FIRST, LEARN HOW TO SPOT ONE - THEY ARE OFTEN THIN, PALE AND HAVE 'LIVED' FOR CENTURIES, SO ARE USUALLY VERY WELL DRESSED.

ARE YOU A VAMPIRE?

NO, I'M JUST COOL.

NEXT, GATHER THE FOLLOWING ITEMS TO BATTLE ONE:

CLOVES OF GARLIC - VAMPIRES HATE THE STUFF!

BODY ARMOUR - TO MAKE YOUR SKIN FANG-PROOF.

A CRUCIFIX WILL FREAK VAMPIRES OUT.

A HOCKEY STICK - BEHEAD A VAMPIRE WITH ONE OF THESE TO KILL IT.

A SHARPENED SILVER STAKE - A STAB THROUGH A VAMPIRE'S HEART WILL KILL IT. AVOID A WOODEN STAKE - ONCE THEY ROT, THE VAMPIRE CAN RETURN TO LIFE!

MATCHES AND CANDLES - VAMPIRES WILL BURN TO ASH IF SET ALIGHT.

HOLY WATER - THIS BURNS THEIR SKIN.

HOW TO SURVIVE A TORNADO

TORNADOS ARE FUNNELS OF VIOLENT, SPINNING AIR THAT COME OUT OF THUNDERSTORMS. READ ON TO FIND OUT WHAT TO DO IF ONE HITS.

IF YOU CAN, GET INSIDE A BUILDING AND GO TO THE LOWEST LEVEL - A BASEMENT IS IDEAL.

IF THERE'S NO BASEMENT, FIND A HALLWAY OR INSIDE UTILITY ROOM.

CROUCH UNDER A STURDY PIECE OF FURNITURE, FAR AWAY FROM ANY WINDOWS THAT MIGHT SHATTER IN THE WIND.

PROTECT YOUR HEAD WITH YOUR HANDS AND ARMS.

IF THERE'S NO STURDY FURNITURE, BUILD A SHELTER OUT OF MATTRESSES AND PROTECT YOUR HEAD WITH A HELMET, IF YOU CAN.

IF YOU CAN'T GET INSIDE A BUILDING IN TIME, RUN AWAY FROM TEMPORARY STRUCTURES THAT COULD BE PICKED UP BY THE TORNADO.

AVOID AREAS WITH LOTS OF TREES AND CARS. QUICKLY FIND A DITCH AND LIE DOWN FLAT UNTIL THE STORM PASSES.

IF YOU'RE IN A CAR WHEN A TORNADO STRIKES, GET OUT AND RUN TO THE CLOSEST BUILDING.

IF THERE ARE NO BUILDINGS, DRIVE AWAY FROM THE TORNADO AT A 90° ANGLE.

AVOID CROSSING ANY BRIDGES AND DON'T PARK IN UNDERPASSES - THEY DON'T OFFER MUCH PROTECTION.

IF THE TORNADO REACHES YOU, GET OUT OF THE CAR AND LIE FLAT IN A DITCH. COVER YOUR FACE AND EYES TO PROTECT THEM FROM FLYING DEBRIS.

HOW TO SURVIVE QUICKSAND

QUICKSAND IS SAND THAT IS SATURATED WITH WATER. IT'S USUALLY ONLY A METRE DEEP BUT YOUR LOWER BODY CAN GET WEDGED WITHIN IT, MAKING IT HARD TO ESCAPE. READ ON TO FIND OUT HOW TO AVOID A STICKY, SANDY END.

OKAY, TEAM, TREAD CAREFULLY. QUICKSAND COULD BE ANYWHERE AROUND HERE.

STAY ALERT IN MARSHY, COASTAL AREAS OR BEACHES WITH STRONG TIDES – THAT'S WHERE YOU CAN FIND DANGEROUS QUICKSAND.

USE A LONG STICK TO PROD THE GROUND IN FRONT OF YOU – IF YOU FEEL IT GETTING STUCK, WARN OTHERS.

CAREFUL, GUYS, QUICKSAND OVER HERE!

IF YOU START SINKING, DON'T PANIC AND THRASH AROUND. THE MORE YOU PANIC, THE MORE YOU WILL SINK.

I THINK I'VE FOUND SOME MORE ...

IF YOU GET STUCK, THROW AWAY HEAVY EQUIPMENT AND LIE BACK AS FLAT AND QUICKLY AS YOU CAN. THIS WILL STOP YOU SINKING FURTHER.

BE CAREFUL NOT TO GET DRAGGED IN, TOO, GUYS!

PUT YOUR STICK UNDER YOUR BACK TO HELP YOU FLOAT. MOVE YOUR FEET IN SMALL CIRCLES TO PADDLE TO SAFETY.

IF YOU CAN'T WRIGGLE FREE, GET SOMEONE TO THROW YOU A ROPE AND HAUL YOU OUT.

NO ROPE? USE A BELT OR UNCLIP THE STRAPS FROM YOUR BACKPACK AND TIE THEM TOGETHER.

IF YOU'RE TOTALLY STUCK, DIG AROUND YOUR BODY TO REDUCE THE SUCTION. ADD WATER TO MAKE THE SAND THINNER AND EASIER TO MOVE IN, UNTIL YOU ARE ABLE TO FLOAT FREE.

HOW TO SURVIVE A SWARM OF BEES

THE GOOD NEWS ABOUT BEES ... IS THAT THEY GENERALLY DON'T GO CHASING AFTER PEOPLE ON PURPOSE.

THE BAD NEWS ABOUT BEES ... IS THAT IF YOU SEE A SWARM HEADING TOWARDS YOU, YOU'RE PROBABLY NEAR THEIR HIVE.

UH, OH!

TO SURVIVE AN ATTACK YOU WILL NEED TO MOVE AND THINK FAST.

DO COVER YOUR MOUTH AND NOSE WITH YOUR SHIRT. THIS WILL STOP THE BEES STINGING THESE SENSITIVE AREAS. IF YOU'VE GOT SUNGLASSES, PUT THEM ON.

DO HEAD INSIDE A BUILDING, A CAR OR A TENT IF YOU ARE NEAR ONE, AND COVER YOURSELF WITH A BLANKET IF YOU CAN.

DO RUN AS FAST AS YOU CAN AWAY FROM THE SWARM.

DON'T SWAT AT THE BEES - THEY ARE ATTRACTED TO MOVEMENT.

DON'T HEAD BACK TO THE HIVE.

DON'T DIVE INTO WATER - THE SWARM MAY HOVER ABOVE AND ATTACK WHEN YOU SURFACE.

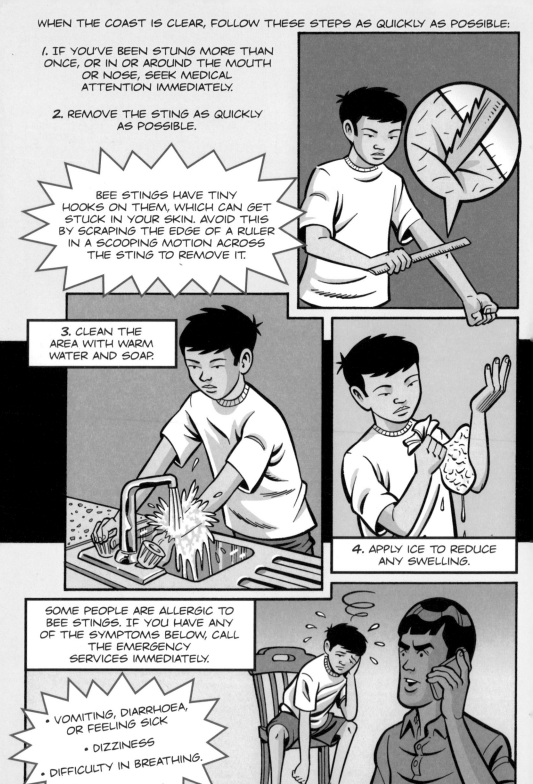

IF YOU NEED TO GO OUTSIDE THE SPACECRAFT, FOLLOW THESE RULES TO STAY SAFE.

1. PUT ON YOUR LIFE-SAVING SPACE SUIT.

FACT: A PACK SUPPLIES YOU WITH OXYGEN AND KEEPS THE SUIT COOL.

FACT: THE HELMET HAS A LIGHT, SO YOU CAN SEE IN SPACE AND A VIDEO CAMERA THAT FILMS WHAT YOU SEE FOR THE CREW BACK ON THE CRAFT.

FACT: THE SUIT PROVIDES YOUR BODY WITH PRESSURE TO KEEP YOUR INSIDES FROM MOVING AROUND ALL OVER THE PLACE.

FACT: THE SUIT SHELL WITHSTANDS ULTRAVIOLET RADIATION, AS WELL AS TEMPERATURES THAT CAN GO FROM 120°C TO -100°C.

2. WEAR YOUR SUIT FOR A FEW HOURS BEFORE LEAVING THE SPACECRAFT - YOUR BODY NEEDS TO BREATHE OUT ALL THE NITROGEN, WHICH CAN CAUSE PAINFUL BUBBLES TO BUILD UP IN YOUR BLOODSTREAM ON A SPACEWALK.

3. TAKE A BUDDY - IT'S SAFER TO SPACEWALK WITH ANOTHER ASTRONAUT WHO CAN OFFER YOU HELP QUICKLY.

ARE YOU OKAY IN THERE?

Also Available:

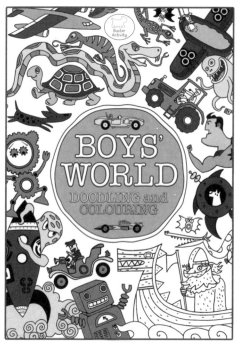

**Boys' World
Doodling and Colouring**
ISBN: 978-1-907151-68-2

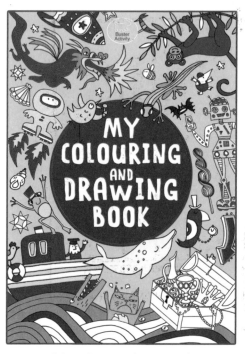

**My Colouring and
Drawing Book**
ISBN: 978-1-78055-012-1

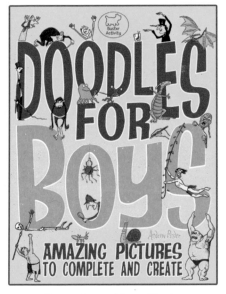

Doodles For Boys
ISBN: 978-1-78055-019-0

The Boys' Handbook
ISBN: 978-1-907151-11-8